Chicago – The B[est]

ISBN 0-7935-7080-8

HAL•LEONARD® CORPORATION

7777 W. BLUEMOUND RD. P.O. BOX 13819 MILWAUKEE, WI 53213

Visit Hal Leonard Online at
www.halleonard.com

Chicago – The Ballads

Contents

AT THE SUNRISE

Words and Music by
ROBERT LAMM

hey, hey, hey, hey.

The

BABY WHAT A BIG SURPRISE

Words and Music by
PETER CETERA

Repeat and Fade

COLOUR MY WORLD

Words and Music by
JAMES PANKOW

Moderately

As time goes on, _____ I re-al-

I DON'T WANNA LIVE
WITHOUT YOUR LOVE

Words and Music by DIANE WARREN
and ALBERT HAMMOND

D.S. al Coda

been a - lone, __ and ba - by, I can't be a - lone now an - y long - er. I don't wan-na

CODA

live my life __ with you. __ Oh, if I had to make it on __ my own, my life would

nev - er be the same, my love _____ would nev - er be the same. __ I don't wan-na

live with - out __ your love. __
Instrumental solo

HARD HABIT TO BREAK

Words and Music by JOHN LEWIS PARK
and STEPHEN KIPI

MCA music publishing

HARD TO SAY I'M SORRY

Words and Music by PETER CETERA
and DAVID FOSTER

(I'VE BEEN)
SEARCHIN' SO LONG

Words and Music by
JAMES PANKOW

Moderately

nat - 'ral, good things __ in life __ take a long __ time. __

IF SHE WOULD HAVE BEEN FAITHFUL

Words and Music by STEPHEN A. KIPNER
and RANDY GOODRUM

IF YOU LEAVE ME NOW

Words and Music by
PETER CETERA

row comes, ___ then we'll both ___ re - gret ___ the things we said ___ to - day.

To Coda

If you leave me now, _____ you'll

take a- way the big - gest part _____ of me. _____ Ooh, _____

_____ no, _____ ba - by, please _____ don't go. _____

LOOK AWAY

Words and Music by
DIANE WARREN

LOVE ME TOMORROW

Words and Music by PETER CETERA
and DAVID FOSTER

NO TELL LOVER

**Words and Music by LEE LOUGHNANE
DANNY SERAPHINE and PETER CETERA**

Pret-ty smile, love-ly face and a warm breeze,

now I need you, la - dy. You're my no tell lov - er.

WE CAN LAST FOREVER

Words and Music by JASON SCHEFF
and JOHN DEXTER

POEM FOR THE PEOPLE

Words and Music by
ROBERT LAMM

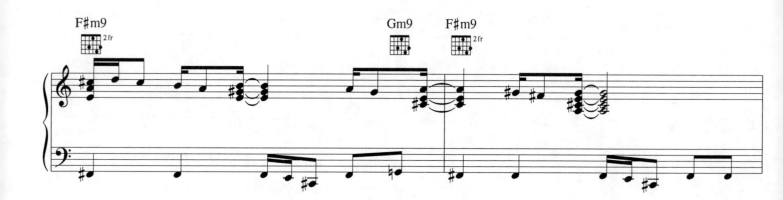

STAY THE NIGHT

Words and Music by PETER CETERA
and DAVID FOSTER

one thing I can tell you, and per-fect-ly clear, we're gon-na have a ver-y good time.

Guitar solo-ad lib.

Solo ends

Stay the night.___ There's room e - nough here for two.___

Lead vocal-ad lib.

Stay the night. ___ I'd like to spend it with you. ____

Stay the night. ___ Why don't we call it a day? ___

Repeat ad lib. and Fade

No one can stop us and noth-ing is in ___ the way. ___

WHAT ELSE CAN I SAY

Words and Music by
PETER CETERA

WHAT KIND OF MAN WOULD I BE?

Words and Music by JASON SCH
CHAS SANDFORD and BOBBY CALDW

WHERE DO WE GO FROM HERE

Words and Music by
PETER CETERA

WISHING YOU WERE HERE

Words and Music by
PETER CETERA

YOU'RE THE INSPIRATION

Words and Music by PETER CETERA
and DAVID FOSTER

Additional Lyrics

2. And I know (yes, I know)
   That it's plain to see
   We're so in love when we're together.
   Now I know (now I know)
   That I need you here with me
   From tonight until the end of time.
   You should know everywhere I go;
   Always on my mind, you're in my heart, in my soul.
   (To Chorus:)